A Note From Rick Renner

I am on a personal quest to see a "revival of the Bible" so people can establish their lives on a firm foundation that will stand strong and endure the test as end-time storm winds begin to intensify.

In order to experience a revival of the Bible in your personal life, it is important to take time each day to read, receive, and apply its truths to your life. James tells us that if we will continue in the perfect law of liberty — refusing to be forgetful hearers, but determined to be doers — we will be blessed in our ways. As you watch or listen to the programs in this series and work through this corresponding study guide, I trust you will search the Scriptures and allow the Holy Spirit to help you hear something new from God's Word that applies specifically to your life. I encourage you to be a doer of the Word He reveals to you. Whatever the cost, I assure you — it will be worth it.

> Thy words were found, and I did eat them;
> and thy word was unto me the joy and rejoicing of mine heart:
> for I am called by thy name, O Lord God of hosts.
> — Jeremiah 15:16

Your brother and friend in Jesus Christ,

Rick Renner

More Questions & Answers With Rick Renner

Copyright © 2021 by Rick Renner
P.O. Box 702040
Tulsa, OK 74170

Published by Rick Renner Ministries
www.renner.org

ISBN 13: 978-1-68031-951-4

eBook ISBN 13: 978-1-68031-952-1

How To Use This Study Guide

This five-lesson study guide corresponds to *"More Questions & Answers With Rick Renner"* (Renner TV). Each lesson in this study guide covers a topic that is addressed during the program series, with questions and references supplied to draw you deeper into your own private study of the Scriptures on this subject.

To derive the most benefit from this study guide, consider the following:

First, watch or listen to the program prior to working through the corresponding lesson in this guide. (Programs can also be viewed at **renner.org** by clicking on the Media/Archives links.)

Second, take the time to look up the scriptures included in each lesson. Prayerfully consider their application to your own life.

Third, use a journal or notebook to make note of your answers to each lesson's Study Questions and Practical Application challenges.

Fourth, invest specific time in prayer and in the Word of God to consult with the Holy Spirit. Write down the scriptures or insights He reveals to you.

Finally, take action! Whatever the Lord tells you to do according to His Word, do it.

For added insights on this subject, it is recommended that you obtain Rick Renner's autobiography *Unlikely: Our Faith-Filled Journey to the Ends of the Earth*. You may also select from Rick's other available resources by placing your order at **renner.org** or by calling 1-800-742-5593.

TOPIC
End-Time Events Questions

SCRIPTURES

1. **Matthew 24:8** — All these are the beginning of sorrows.

2. **Matthew 24:14** — And this gospel of the kingdom shall be preached in all the world for a witness unto all nations; and then shall the end come.

3. **2 Thessalonians 2:3** — Let no man deceive you by any means: for that day shall not come, except there come a falling away first, and that man of sin be revealed, the son of perdition.

4. **Luke 21:11** — And great earthquakes shall be in divers places, and famines, and pestilences; and fearful sights and great signs shall there be from heaven.

5. **Romans 14:10** — …For we shall all stand before the judgment seat of Christ.

6. **Revelation 20:12** — And I saw the dead, small and great, stand before God; and the books were opened: and another book was opened, which is the book of life: and the dead were judged out of those things which were written in the books, according to their works.

7. **Revelation 20:15** — And whosoever was not found written in the book of life was cast into the lake of fire.

8. **Matthew 24:3,4** — And as he sat upon the mount of Olives, the disciples came unto him privately, saying, Tell us, when shall these things be? and what shall be the sign of thy coming, and of the end of the world? And Jesus answered and said unto them, Take heed that no man deceive you.

9. **Joel 2:28,29** — And it shall come to pass afterward, that I will pour out my spirit upon all flesh; and your sons and your daughters shall prophesy, your old men shall dream dreams, your young men shall see visions: And also upon the servants and upon the handmaids in those days will I pour out my spirit.

GREEK WORDS

There are no Greek words included in this lesson.

SYNOPSIS

The five lessons in this study titled *More Questions & Answers With Rick Renner* will focus on the following topics:

- End-Time Events Questions
- Faith and Doctrinal Questions
- Questions Relating to the Supernatural
- Questions About Prayer
- Random Questions

In the studio offices of Renner Ministries in Moscow, Russia, is a beautiful piece of Russian, black-lacquered art called a triptych. It's made of sixteen layers of papier-mache that was formed and then intricately hand painted by an artist and features detailed scenes of Russian fairy tales. These depictions are quite exquisite and are painted with a brush that has one hair!

The interesting thing about these hand-painted, fairytale scenes is that the men who painted them are the same professional artists who masterfully painted biblical artworks in Russian churches before the Bolshevik Revolution took place. When communism came in and took over, society changed, causing the beliefs and trends to be modified. Thus, these skilled artists went from illustrating the true history of Scripture to illustrating Russian fairy tales.

This is a vivid reminder of what the Holy Spirit prophesied would take place in the last of the last days. Through the apostle Paul, the Spirit warns us that at the very end of the age, people will turn away from listening to the truth and begin listening to fables (*see* 2 Timothy 4:4). And that's what we see happening all around us today. People who once loved and embraced the truth of Scripture are gravitating toward and seeking out things that don't line up with God's Word.

In this lesson, we will answer some of your questions regarding end-time events and what our response to them should be.

The emphasis of this lesson:

In this lesson, Rick answers questions like: Are we living in pre-Tribulation times, or are we *in* the Tribulation? What do the words "falling away" in Second Thessalonians 2:3 mean? Does the Bible say anything about UFOs? What is the greatest warning Jesus gave on the Mount of Olives concerning "signs of the last days"? Where in the Bible is it prophesied that a great revival will take place before Jesus comes?

QUESTION 1: Are we living in pre-Tribulation times, or are we living *in* the Tribulation?

No, we are not living in the Tribulation; we are living in the time immediately before it. In Matthew 24, Jesus gives us a list of multiple signs we will see prior to His return and the end of the age. And partway through this list, He said, "All these are *the beginning of sorrows*" (Matthew 24:8). The word "sorrows" here is the Greek word *oodin*, which describes *birth pains* or *the pain of childbirth*. It specifically denotes the *contractions* a woman experiences before she gives birth to her child. Furthermore, this word *oodin* — translated here as "sorrows" — can also describe *the pain necessary to open up or to introduce something new.*

Stop and think about a woman who is about to give birth. At the very beginning of her labor, her contractions are sporadic and spaced out. But as she comes closer and closer to the time of delivery, her contractions increase in number and in intensity. Eventually, they become so frequent and severe that she can no longer discern when one ends and the next one begins. This is her body's way of opening up to bring her new baby into the world.

By using this word "sorrows" — the Greek word *oodin* — Jesus is telling us that before His return and the wrap up of this age, the world and its inhabitants will begin to experience contraction-like pains. The closer and closer we get to the very end, the greater the frequency and intensity of the pains society will be experiencing — just like a woman getting ready to give birth to a child. And once those contractions start, they cannot be stopped.

A careful look at the last 25 years — or just the last 10 years — we can see a dramatic increase in the frequency and intensity of catastrophic occurrences. It seems as though things that used to be rare are now happening one after another after another. Jesus prophesied this would be a major indication that the very end of the age is near. Thus, disastrous events are going to continue occurring more and more and get closer and closer all the way up to His return. In fact, they will become so numerous it will be hard to tell when one ends and the next one begins.

The Ultimate Sign That Jesus' Return Is Eminent

In Matthew 24:14, Jesus went on to say, "And this gospel of the kingdom shall be preached in all the world for a witness unto all nations; and then shall the end come." The word "then" means *exactly then* or *at that precise moment*, which means when the Gospel has been presented everywhere it's supposed to go and every person who is going to repent has repented, then the end will come.

The fact is, most of the world can hear the Gospel today if they choose to hear it. Consider this: the population of the world today is nearly eight billion people, and of that eight billion, it is estimated that there are five billion mobile phones. If someone has a mobile or smart phone, he or she has access to the preaching of the Gospel right in the palm of their hands. Likewise, if a person has a radio, TV, or access to the Internet in some way, he has access to some form of the Gospel. Technology has truly changed everything, making it possible for nearly the whole world to hear the Gospel — and in many cases, to even hear it in their own language.

This worldwide availability of the Gospel has never happened before, and it could only occur at the very end of the age. A better translation of Matthew 24:14 from the original Greek text would be, "When this gospel of the kingdom is preached and heralded to all who are living in the civilized, technologically advanced world as a witness unto all nations; *then shall the end come*." That's where we're living — in the closing moments of the Church age just before the Great Tribulation.

QUESTION 2: Please explain Second Thessalonians 2:3. What do the words "falling away" mean?

The apostle Paul addressed the crisis of worldwide deception in Second Thessalonians 2:3 by issuing this warning: "Let no man deceive you by any means: for that day shall not come, except there come *a falling away* first, and that man of sin be revealed, the son of perdition."

First of all, when Paul talks about "that day," he is referring to the return of Christ. Thus, he says that the rapture of the Church will not take place until there is first a "falling away." In Greek, the phrase "falling away" is a translation of the word *apostasia*, which is where we get the word *apostasy*. It is a compound of the word *apo*, which means *away*, and the word *stasia*, which means *to step*. When these words are compounded to form *apostasia*, it describes *a falling away or revolt*. It is even the word for a *mutiny*.

Before the Great Tribulation takes place, there's going to be a worldwide stepping away from the timeless truth and standards of God's Word. If you look around, you will see this mutinous mindset popping up every-where — even in the Church. This is a major sign that we are very close to Christ's return. On the heels of this great apostasy, Jesus is going to come back to rapture the Church to Himself.

Now some people have tried to say that this "falling away" and the "catch-ing away" — or rapture of the Church — is the same event, but that is not the case. The "falling away" (*apostasia*) is the *stepping away* or *departure from the authority of Scripture*. It is a rebellious, disobedient attitude toward God.

The 'Falling Away' and the 'Departure From the Faith' Are Connected

All throughout the New Testament, the Holy Spirit foretold of the great deception that would come in the Last Days. The apostle Paul voiced this warning in First Timothy 4:1, saying, "Now the Spirit speaketh expressly, that in the latter times some shall depart from the faith, giving heed to seducing spirits and doctrines of devils."

This "departure from the faith" refers to the "falling away" that will take place in the Church. The word "depart" in First Timothy 4:1 is the Greek word *aphistemi*, which means *to stand apart from; to distance one's self from; to step away from*. This word describes *a very gradual withdrawal from something*. In the context of this verse, *it is a very slow, almost imperceptible move away from* "the faith," which refers to *the time-tested truth of Scripture*. It is from this very Greek word that we derive the term *apostate* or *apostasy*.

Paul said this departure from the faith would result from believers "…giving heed to seducing spirits and doctrines of devils" (1 Timothy 4:1). The phrase "giving heed" in Greek is the word *prosecho*, and it means *to hold or embrace*. It pictures *a person who has believed and held on to one thing for a very long time now and is leaning in a new direction believing and embracing something else.* As people depart from the solid truth of God's Word, they will begin to embrace new ideas and concepts not in line with Scripture.

The influencing factor behind this departure from truth will be "seducing spirits." The word "seducing" is the Greek word *planao*, and it describes *deception* or *a moral wandering.* It depicts *a person or nation who has veered from a solid path.* And the word "devils" is the Greek word *daimonion*, which describes *evil spirits, demons,* or *devils.* The ancient world generally believed demons thickly populated the lower regions of the air and that spirits were the primary cause of disasters, suffering, and actions of insanity. In the Last Days, false teaching will become so deceptive and so prevalent it will cause people to morally and spiritually lose their bearings and embrace crazy, insane ideas.

Immediately on the heels of this falling away will be the rapture of the Church, and then the Bible says, "...that man of sin [will] be revealed, the son of perdition" (2 Thessalonians 2:3). The Greek word for "sin" here means *lawlessness.* So *the man of lawlessness* will suddenly be unveiled once the Church is taken out of the way. It is very possible he is alive on the earth waiting in the wings to be revealed. Right now the world is being primed and prepared on all levels to receive this *lawless* one — he is the antichrist who will rule during the Tribulation. To avoid being swept up in deception in these final hours, we need to hold tightly to the truth of God's Word and earnestly contend for the faith that was given to us (*see* Jude 2,3).

QUESTION 3: In light of the government releasing videos of UFOs and what seems like credible stories from the military, what does the Bible say about things coming from the heavens in the last days?

Although the Bible doesn't talk specifically about UFOs, there is a very intriguing statement made by Jesus in Luke 21:11. Regarding the signs we would see before His return, He said, "And great earthquakes shall be in divers places, and famines, and pestilences; and fearful sights and great signs shall there be from heaven." Notice the words "fearful sights." This is a translation of the unusual Greek word *phobetron*, and it describes *monstrous events* or *scary events.* This phrase comes from a Greek word that depicts *fright, horror or something that is scary.* Greek writers usually used this word to describe *monsters.*

Jesus said that *monstrous, scary events* will be accompanied by "great signs," and they shall "be from heaven." In the original Greek, it literally says *from the heavens* or *something descending directly from the sky.* Therefore, the majority of the human race will be aware of these events when they take place. Was Jesus referring to a giant meteor, a solar flare, or some other form of cataclysmic, natural disaster? Is it a horrific scientific development? The Scripture is not clear. Nevertheless, when these great signs come down from the heavens, they will alert us that we're on the precipice of the very, very end of this age and the beginning of the next one.

QUESTION 4: As we enter the last days, what is the greatest warning Jesus gave on the Mount of Olives about "signs of the last days" in Matthew 24?

The fact is Jesus' disciples asked many of the same questions that believers are asking today. For example, the Bible tells us of a time when the disciples gathered around Jesus to talk to Him about the Last Days. Matthew 24:3 says, "And as he sat upon the mount of Olives, the disciples came unto him privately, saying, Tell us, when shall these things be? and what shall be the sign of thy coming, and of the end of the world?"

In Greek, the word "when" describes *specific, concrete information*, and the word "what" describes *minute details.* This tells us that the disciples were saying, "Lord, don't be vague. Tell us specific, concrete information regarding the time of the end. We want to know *precisely*, down to the smallest detail, what will be the sign of Your coming."

This word "sign" is the Greek word *semeion*, and it describes *a marker or sign to alert a traveler to where he is on a road.* It was *an authenticating mark or specific sign* letting one know how much further he had to go to reach his destination. Jesus gave us multiple "signs" to let us know where we are on the prophetic road of time and how much farther we need to go until we reach the end of the age.

The Greatest Warning Jesus Gave

What's interesting is that many people often miss the very first sign Jesus gave. It is found in Matthew 24:4 where He said, "…Take heed that no man deceive you." The phrase "take heed" is a form of the Greek word *blepo*, which means *to watch* or *pay attention.* It is a word used to jar and jolt listeners to sit up, throw their shoulders back, open their ears, and really listen and be attentive to what is being said. What Jesus was getting ready to say was extremely important.

Once He had acquired the disciples' full attention, He unveiled the first and foremost sign we would see that will mark the end of the age. He said, "…Take heed that no man *deceive* you" (Mathew 24:4). The word "deceive" here is a translation of the Greek word *planao*, which means *delusion* and depicts *a deceptive, moral wandering; a people who have veered from a solid path*. Essentially, Jesus said, "When you see worldwide deception and delusion, you'll know that you've come to the end of the age."

[For more on this topic, please check out Rick's book and study guide *Signs You'll See Just Before Jesus Comes*.]

QUESTION 5: It's been said that a great revival will occur before Jesus returns. Where in the Bible is this prophesied?

Through the prophet Joel, God prophesied that there would be a great outpouring of His Holy Spirit all over the world. He said, "And it shall come to pass afterward, that I will pour out my spirit upon all flesh; and your sons and your daughters shall prophesy, your old men shall dream dreams, your young men shall see visions: And also upon the servants and upon the handmaids in those days will I pour out my spirit" (Joel 2:28,29).

This great outpouring began at the beginning of the last days, which was just over 2,000 years ago when the Church was born on the Day of Pentecost. Peter stood up and proclaimed that Joel's prophecy was being fulfilled (*see* Acts 2:16-18). This outpouring of God's Spirit is still taking place in parts of the world today and will continue to intensify right up until the time of the rapture of the Church. Therefore, as we approach Jesus' return, two things will be happening simultaneously: there's going to be this great outpouring of the Holy Spirit and at the same time, a falling away or departure from the faith in the Church.

[For more on this topic, please check out Rick's book and study guide *Last-Days Survival Guide*.]

QUESTION 6: What will the Judgment Seat of Christ be like for believers and unbelievers?

The Bible tells us in Romans 14:10, "…For we shall all stand before the judgment seat of Christ." To be clear: the Judgment Seat of Christ is only for believers and it is not a place where we will be evaluated to see whether or not we are worthy of salvation. If a person has sincerely repented of his sins and invited Jesus to be his Savior and Lord, he is saved and forgiven — period (*see* 1 John 1:9).

The word "judgment" in Romans 14:10 is the Greek word *bema*, which describes *the platform on which the contestants in sporting competitions in the ancient games were awarded by the judges for their performance.* Only believers will stand before the Judgment Seat of Christ, and there our lives will be examined by Jesus Himself and rewarded for the things we did for Him.

Unbelievers will *not* stand before the Judgment Seat of Christ. Instead, they will stand before God's Great White Throne Judgment. This is referred to in Revelation 20:12, which says, "And I saw the dead, small and great, stand before God; and the books were opened: and another book was opened, which is the book of life: and the dead were judged out of those things which were written in the books, according to their works." Verse 15 goes on to say, "And whosoever was not found written in the book of life was cast into the lake of fire."

To be clear, the Great White Throne Judgment is not for believers — it is for unbelievers. The reality of this coming judgment should motivate us to pray for our unsaved family members and friends — for God to give them the measure of faith to believe in and receive Jesus as their Lord and Savior.

STUDY QUESTIONS

Study to shew thyself approved unto God, a workman that needeth not to be ashamed, rightly dividing the word of truth.
— 2 Timothy 2:15

1. Of all the questions and answers presented in this lesson, which one spoke to you the most? Why was it so impactful?
2. In your own words, describe what the Holy Spirit means when He says that there will be a "falling away" before the return of Christ? How is the "falling away" different from the "catching away," or rapture of the Church? In what ways are you seeing this "falling away" happen right now in the world?

3. The Bible tells us in Romans 14:10, "...For we shall all stand before the judgment seat of Christ." According to First Corinthians 3:12-15; 4:5 and Second Corinthians 5:10, what is going to take place at this appointed time for believers?

PRACTICAL APPLICATION

> But be ye doers of the word, and not hearers only,
> deceiving your own selves.
> —James 1:22

1. Jesus said that before His return and the wrap up of this age, the world and its inhabitants will begin to experience contraction-like pains. The closer and closer we get to the very end, the greater the frequency and intensity of the pains society will be experiencing. What are some of the "contractions" (pains) you are seeing in society? How have these events increased in recent years?

2. To avoid being swept up in deception in these last days, we need to hold tightly to the truth of God's Word and earnestly contend for the faith that was given to us (*see* Jude 2,3). Take a moment and pray, *Holy Spirit, what do I need to change in my daily routine in order for me to have more quality time in the Word? Where in the Bible should I be reading and studying? Please teach me Your Word and make it come alive. In Jesus' name. Amen.*

3. The White Throne Judgment is not for believers — it is for unbelievers (*see* Revelation 20:11-15). How does the reality and finality of this coming judgment motivate you to pray for your unsaved family members and friends — for God to give them the measure of faith to believe in and receive Jesus as their Lord and Savior?

TOPIC

Faith and Doctrinal Questions

SCRIPTURES

1. **Hebrews 6:12** — That ye be not slothful, but followers of them who through faith and patience inherit the promises.

2. **Hebrews 10:36** — For ye have need of patience, that, after ye have done the will of God, ye might receive the promise.

3. **Hebrews 12:1** — Wherefore seeing we also are compassed about with so great a cloud of witnesses, let us lay aside every weight, and the sin which doth so easily beset us, and let us run with patience the race that is set before us.

4. **Isaiah 53:4,5** — Surely he hath borne our griefs, and carried our sorrows: yet we did esteem him stricken, smitten of God, and afflicted. But he was wounded for our transgressions, he was bruised for our iniquities: the chastisement of our peace was upon him; and with his stripes we are healed.

5. **Matthew 8:16** — When the even was come, they brought unto him many that were possessed with devils: and he cast out the spirits with his word, and healed all that were sick.

6. **Matthew 8:17** — That it might be fulfilled which was spoken by Esaias the prophet, saying, Himself took our infirmities, and bare our sicknesses.

7. **Luke 16:9** — And I say unto you, Make to yourselves friends of the mammon of unrighteousness; that, when ye fail, they may receive you into everlasting habitations.

8. **Ephesians 1:7** — In whom we have redemption through his blood, the forgiveness of sins, according to the riches of his grace.

9. **Hebrews 2:3** — …so great salvation….

10. **1 Timothy 1:4** — Neither give heed to fables and endless genealogies, which minister questions, rather than godly edifying which is in faith: so do.

11. **Matthew 19:14** — But Jesus said, Suffer little children, and forbid them not, to come unto me: for of such is the kingdom of heaven.

12. **Romans 10:9,10** — That if thou shalt confess with thy mouth the Lord Jesus, and shalt believe in thine heart that God hath raised him from the dead, thou shalt be saved. For with the heart man believeth unto righteousness; and with the mouth confession is made unto salvation.

GREEK WORDS

There are no Greek words included in this lesson.

SYNOPSIS

Many people have questions about the armor of God described by the apostle Paul in Ephesians 6. For instance, research reveals that every Roman soldier had seven pieces of weaponry. Six of these pieces are identifiable in Ephesians 6:13-18, but it seems that one piece — the soldier's spear — is missing.

A closer look at Ephesians 6:18 reveals that the spear is indeed there. Here, Paul says we are to be, "Praying always with all prayer and supplication in the Spirit…." The Greek literally says, "Pray always with all kinds of prayer." What did Paul have in his mind?

Well, as part of the Roman soldier's arsenal, he had a pouch on the backside of his armor that held several different kinds of spears or lances. Some of them were short, others were long, and some were between the two sizes. He even had one spear that was 24 feet long. A soldier who knew how to use his spear could hurl it at the enemy and deal with him from a distance. This prevented the enemy from ever getting too close.

In the same way, we as believers have been given several different kinds of prayer to use in our fight against the enemy. We could call this our *spear of influence*. Prayer is not a "one-size-fits all" weapon. If we will learn how to use the right prayer at the right time, we too can effectively deal with the devil from a distance so he never gets too close.

The emphasis of this lesson:

In this lesson, Rick answers questions like: How do we go from believing to receiving God's promises? What does Hebrews 12:1 mean when it says we're surrounded by "so great a cloud of witnesses"? Did Jesus really take our sicknesses and diseases when He died on the Cross? What

did He mean when He said, "...Make friends for yourselves by means of unrighteous wealth" (Luke 16:9)? Are extra-biblical books, such as the book of Enoch, to be taken seriously? And can young children really be saved?

QUESTION 1: How do you go from believing to receiving the promises of God?

In Hebrews 6:12, the Bible says, "That ye be not slothful, but followers of them who through faith and patience inherit the promises." In this verse we see that it takes both *faith* and *patience* to inherit the promises of God. Faith is an *initiator*, and it is always acting and moving forward. In fact, the word faith in Greek is usually used in a masculine way. Patience, on the other hand, is feminine. Isn't that interesting? Just as it takes a man and a woman to come together to produce a child, *it takes faith and patience to come together to give birth to the promises of God.*

Hebrews 10:36 goes on to say, "For ye have need of patience, that, after ye have done the will of God, ye might receive the promise." This verse guarantees that we're going to receive the promise, but we need patience to see it become a reality. The word "patience" here is the Greek word *hupomone*, which means *to stay* or *to abide*. It means *to remain in one's spot; to keep a position;* or *to resolve to maintain territory that has been gained.* It has been described as *staying power* or *hang-in-there power.* It is *the attitude that holds out, holds on, outlasts, perseveres, and hangs in there, never giving up, refusing to surrender to obstacles, and turning down every opportunity to quit.*

Again, the Bible says, "...After ye have done the will of God, ye might receive the promise" (Hebrews 10:36). The word "receive" here is the Greek word *komidzo*, which means *to receive what is due* or *to receive what one has coming to him.* It could be translated as *payday.* This lets us know payday will come to anyone who stands in faith — believing and tenaciously waiting in patience for it to come to pass.

So if it seems like it's taking a long time to see God's promise fulfilled, don't be discouraged. Stay in faith and keep planting into patience, and you'll see the promise of God manifest in your life.

[For more on this topic, please check out Rick's five-part series *The Stage of Faith.*]

QUESTION 2: Please explain the meaning of Hebrews 12 that says we are compassed with "so great a cloud of witnesses."

In Hebrews 12:1, it says, "Wherefore seeing we also are compassed about with so great a cloud of witnesses, let us lay aside every weight, and the sin which doth so easily beset us, and let us run with patience the race that is set before us."

The key to understanding this verse is in the meaning of the word "cloud." In Greek, it is the word *nephos*, and while it describes *white, fluffy clouds* we see in the sky, it also carries a deeper meaning. In classical Greek, the word "cloud" (*nephos*) described *the highest seats in the bleachers of a stadium or coliseum.* And the seats at the very top were called *the clouds* because they were so high up in the air. When you came into a coliseum or a stadium, you could buy seats down on the lower level, which was closer to where the game was being played. But as all the lower and middle seats kept filling up, eventually the last seats available would be the ones in the clouds.

By using this word "cloud," the writer of Hebrews is saying, "Hey, it's your turn to play the game. You're on the playing field now, and surrounding you in the grandstands of Heaven all the way to the very top are all the godly people who've lived before you. They're watching from *the clouds.* Just as they received a word from God, faced the impossible, and received by faith what they were believing for, so can you! They are proof that you can make it too."

Friend, we're in the middle of the arena, and this is our moment to play the game. So let's play it well and give God everything we've got.

[For more on this topic, please check out Rick's ten-part series *God's Hall of Faith.*]

QUESTION 3: Did Jesus really take our sicknesses and diseases when He died on the Cross?

This is a very important question. The Bible says in Isaiah 53:4 and 5, "Surely he hath borne our griefs, and carried our sorrows: yet we did esteem him stricken, smitten of God, and afflicted. But he was wounded for our transgressions, he was bruised for our iniquities: the chastisement of our peace was upon him; and with his stripes we are healed."

Now you may have heard it taught that this verse refers to spiritual healing — that when Jesus died on the Cross, His sacrifice paid for our spiritual healing. Well, according to Scripture, before we were saved, our spirits were "...dead in trespasses and sins" (Ephesians 2:1). What is dead can't be healed; it can only be *resurrected*, which is exactly what God did.

Ephesians 2:5 and 6 says, "Even when we were dead in sins, [God] hath quickened us together with Christ, (by grace ye are saved;) And hath raised us up together, and made us sit together in heavenly places in Christ Jesus." The word "quickened" in verse 5 means *to make alive*. That is what God did. He made our spirit, which was dead, *alive again* and raised us up — resurrected us — in Christ Jesus!

When the Bible says, "...With his stripes we are healed" (Isaiah 53:5), it means we are *physically healed*. Those were the griefs and sorrows Jesus bore on our behalf. This is confirmed in the gospels. Matthew 8:16 says, "When the even was come, they brought unto him many that were possessed with devils: and he cast out the spirits with his word, and healed all that were sick." The word "brought" here is the Greek word *phero*, and it means *to physically carry*. These people were so sick they needed to be carried to where Jesus was.

Moreover, the phrase "possessed with devils" is the Greek word *daimonid-zomai*, and it describes *those that were demonized* or *those under the influence of a demon or group of demons*. The tense here indicates *a chronic case of demonization*. The Bible says with His word, Jesus "cast out the spirits." In Greek, the words "cast out" is the word *ekballo*, which means *to forcibly evict; to throw out; to cast out; to expel; to drive out; to kick out*. Historically, this word was used to describe *a nation that forcibly deported lawbreakers from its borders*. Jesus evicted these demons from the lives of the people.

And then it says Jesus "healed" them, which in this verse is the Greek word *therapeuo*. It's where we get the word *therapy*, and it pictures *a healing touch that requires corresponding actions*. In other words, Jesus didn't just touch people and send them on their way. He required them to do something to demonstrate that they were healed. If the person had a withered hand, He commanded them to stretch it forth. If they couldn't walk and were confined to a mat, He told them to pick up their mat and walk. In all the gospels, the word *therapeuo* is the primary word used to describe the healing ministry of Jesus.

It's very interesting to note that the very next verse in Matthew's gospel confirms Isaiah 53:4,5. Matthew 8:17 says, "That it might be fulfilled which was spoken by Esaias [Isaiah] the prophet, saying, Himself took our infirmities, and bare our sicknesses." Indeed, by the stripes Jesus received from the beating to His body, we are physically healed! Physical healing has been paid for by Christ and it belongs to you. Claim it by faith for yourself and your loved ones.

[For more on this topic, please check out Rick's 15-part series *The Miracles of Jesus Christ*.]

QUESTION 4: What did Jesus mean when he said, "…Make to yourselves friends of the mammon of unrighteousness; that, when ye fail, they may receive you into everlasting habitations" (Luke 16:9).

In Luke 16:9, the word "mammon" is the word *mamonas*, which is a very old Greek word that denotes *money* or *wealth*. When the words "mammon of unrighteousness" are used together, it depicts *common, worldly money,* along with all of its buying power in this earthly realm.

Thus when Jesus said, "…Make to yourselves friends of the mammon of unrighteousness; that, when ye fail, they may receive you into everlasting habitations" (Luke 16:9), He's basically telling us, "If you use your common, earthly money for the preaching of the Gospel, when you fail — or pass away and enter eternity — you will make forever friends." Who are these friends? They are people who repented and made Jesus their Lord and Savior as a result of the finances you gave. When you die, they're going to be waiting in Heaven to receive you with gratefulness for what you gave!

[For more on this topic, please check out Rick's book *A Life Ablaze*.]

QUESTION 5: Can you please address the teachings on generational curses. It seems some people don't understand redemption and claim as a child of God, there can be generational curses still on you. I can't find anywhere that this is biblical.

Understanding redemption through Jesus Christ is key to experiencing supernatural rest in Him. Through His finished work, Jesus broke every curse of sin. Ephesians 1:7 says, "In whom we have redemption through his blood, the forgiveness of sins, according to the riches of his grace." The Greek word for "redemption" in this verse is *apolutrosis*, and it is the picture of *a slave being purchased out of a slave market*.

Specifically, this word *apolutrosis* — translated here as "redemption" — means that Jesus paid the ransom in order to *return* us to the condition we were in *before* our captivity began. In the plainest of language, this means that Jesus paid the price to *permanently set us free* and to *restore* us to the full status of sons and daughters of God!

When Jesus came into our lives and His blood was applied to us, it broke all curses and all forms of bondage. The apostle Paul declared, "Christ hath redeemed us from the curse of the law, being made a curse for us: for it is written, Cursed is every one that hangeth on a tree" (Galatians 3:13).

Friend, don't minimize your salvation. In Christ you are free! Jesus paid the price for your redemption, and you can rest in it. Your salvation is not a small redemption, but a great one. Embrace its fullness and learn how to release it in your life. Christ has set you free from generational curses.

[For more on this topic, please check out Rick's five-part series *Resting in Our Redemption*.]

QUESTION 6: Can young children really be saved and baptized? Can they really understand their need for Jesus?

Children are very important and valuable to Jesus. In Matthew 19:14, "…Jesus said, Suffer little children, and forbid them not, to come unto me: for of such is the kingdom of heaven." And in Luke18:17, He said, "…Whosoever shall not receive the kingdom of God as a little child shall in no wise enter therein."

Children are precious to God, and in many ways it's easier for them to believe and put their faith in Him at a young age than an adult. Nowhere in Scripture is there an age limit for when someone can come to Christ. The only requirements given are in Romans 10:9 and 10, which says, "…If thou shalt confess with thy mouth the Lord Jesus, and shalt believe in thine heart that God hath raised him from the dead, thou shalt be saved. For with the heart man believeth unto righteousness; and with the mouth confession is made unto salvation."

Here we find there are two actions required in salvation:

1. You have to believe in your heart that Jesus is Lord and that God raised Him from the dead. With the heart, we believe unto righteousness. Like Abraham, our faith is credited to us as righteousness (*see* Romans 4:3).

2. You also have to confess that Jesus is Lord with your mouth. With the mouth confession is made to salvation. Remember, out of the abundance of what's in your heart, your mouth will speak (*see* Luke 6:45). It's not enough to think it — you have to *confess* it. And the moment you confess Jesus is Lord, the gift of salvation explodes on the inside of you!

QUESTION 7: Are extra-biblical books, such as the book of Enoch, authentic and to be taken seriously?

A number of people are asking this question today, especially about the book of Enoch. We know from Scripture that Jesus, the apostle Paul, and Jude all quoted from the book of Enoch. It also seems that the book of Revelation alludes to the book of Enoch. Although the book of Enoch is a historical book, it is not a biblical book, and we must keep that in mind.

There are a number of books that were written in the Second, Third, and Fourth Centuries that were just fictional, false books — sometimes referred to as pseudo-epistles, and we can't put any stock in them. In fact, they fall into the category of what the apostle Paul wrote about in First Timothy 1:4, where he said, "Neither give heed to fables and endless genealogies, which minister questions, rather than godly edifying which is in faith: so do."

Friend, if you have the Bible, you have the full counsel of God. It is complete and lacking nothing. Don't get caught up spending your precious time worrying about all those extra-biblical books. Stick with Scripture.

STUDY QUESTIONS

Study to shew thyself approved unto God, a workman that needeth not to be ashamed, rightly dividing the word of truth.
— 2 Timothy 2:15

1. As you think about the seven questions addressed in this lesson, which one impacted you most? Why is it so meaningful?

2. Jesus really did take *your* sicknesses and diseases when He died on the Cross. To keep you from struggling to believe His physical healing is

available to you, take time to carefully meditate on these promises He made and begin to speak them out over your life.

- **"God *wants* to heal me."** – Matthew 8:1-3; Mark 1:40-42; Luke 5:12,13; 3 John 2

- **"Through Jesus *I am healed.*"** – Matthew 8:17; Isaiah 53:4,5 and 1 Peter 2:24

- **"God is *well-able* to heal me."** – Matthew 19:26; Luke 1:37; Jeremiah 32:27;Ephesians 3:20

PRACTICAL APPLICATION

But be ye doers of the word, and not hearers only,
deceiving your own selves.
—James 1:22

1. What promise has God spoken to your heart through His Word and/ or by His Spirit that you're holding onto tenaciously? How is He using the difficult situation (or situations) you're in to stretch and strengthen your faith and build patience into your character?

2. In Christ you are free! Jesus paid a high price for your full redemption on the Cross. Galatians 3:13 declares, "Christ hath redeemed us from the curse of the law, being made a curse for us…." In what areas of your life are you experiencing the greatest levels of freedom? Where does freedom seem to be eluding you? Begin to proclaim this promise daily over every area of your life: "Christ has redeemed me from the curse of the law…sin no longer has dominion over me" (Galatians 3:13; Romans 6:14).

3. God's Word tells us not to "…give heed to fables and endless geneal-ogies, which cause disputes rather than godly edification which is in faith" (1 Timothy 1:4 *NKJV*). Be honest: Have you gotten caught up wasting your precious time arguing and worrying about things that have no eternal value? What things do you know you need to let go of and walk away from so that you can give your full attention to God's Word?

TOPIC

Questions Relating to the Supernatural

SCRIPTURES

1. **1 Peter 4:10** — As every man hath received the gift, even so minister the same one to another, as good stewards of the manifold grace of God.

2. **Acts 2:17** — And it shall come to pass in the last days, saith God, I will pour out of my Spirit upon all flesh: and your sons and your daughters shall prophesy, and your young men shall see visions, and your old men shall dream dreams.

3. **Acts 8:38-40** — And he commanded the chariot to stand still: and they went down both into the water, both Philip and the eunuch; and he baptized him. And when they were come up out of the water, the Spirit of the Lord caught away Philip, that the eunuch saw him no more: and he went on his way rejoicing. But Philip was found at Azotus: and passing through he preached in all the cities, till he came to Caesarea.

4. **Acts 14:19,20** — And there came thither certain Jews from Antioch and Iconium, who persuaded the people, and, having stoned Paul, drew him out of the city, supposing he had been dead. Howbeit, as the disciples stood round about him, he rose up, and came into the city: and the next day he departed with Barnabas to Derbe.

5. **2 Corinthians 12:1-4** — It is not expedient for me doubtless to glory. I will come to visions and revelations of the Lord. I knew a man in Christ above fourteen years ago, (whether in the body, I cannot tell; or whether out of the body, I cannot tell: God knoweth;) such an one caught up to the third heaven. And I knew such a man, (whether in the body, or out of the body, I cannot tell: God knoweth;) How that he was caught up into paradise, and heard unspeakable words, which it is not lawful for a man to utter.

6. **Ephesians 6:12** — For we wrestle not against flesh and blood, but against principalities, against powers, against the rulers of the darkness of this world, against spiritual wickedness in high places.

GREEK WORDS

There are no Greek words included in this lesson.

SYNOPSIS

In 1978, when Rick Renner was still a teenager, God spoke to his heart and told him, "Write, write, write. I will prosper what you write." Rick has obeyed God's calling, and the Lord has prospered everything he has written. He did his part in the natural, and God blessed it with His supernatural power.

What has God asked *you* to do? Do you know? How has He gifted you to represent Him and help others connect with Jesus? If you'll do your part, He will certainly do His. The Bible says we are called to *plant* and to *water*, but it is God and only God who brings the fruitful increase (*see* 1 Corinthians 3:7,8). If you'll be obedient, He will bless the work of your hands and minister to others through you in ways you have never dreamed!

The emphasis of this lesson:

In Lesson 3, Rick answers questions like: How can I begin to operate in the gifts of the Spirit? Can people really be translated in the spirit from one place to another? Specifically, is it biblical for a person to visit Heaven? Are there evil spirits over regions and cities? If so, what authority do we have to pull them down and to do warfare against them? And how can I detect a demon in someone I love and cast it out of him or her?

QUESTION 1: How can I begin to operate in the gifts of the Spirit and do it often?

God wants each and every one of us — His children — to operate in the gifts of the Holy Spirit. First Peter 4:10 confirms this saying, "As every man hath received the gift, even so minister the same one to another, as good stewards of the manifold grace of God."

The word "gift" here is the Greek word *charisma*, and its use lets us know this verse is not talking about natural talents. The word *charisma* is from the Greek word *charis*, which is the Greek word for *grace*. These "gifts" are *grace-given endowments* that are supernatural in origin and operation, and the moment you're born again you have the ability to function in them.

Notice Peter said, "As every man hath received the gift..." (1 Peter 4:10). In Greek, the words "every man" are a translation of the word *hekastos*, which is an all-inclusive term that embraces *everyone, with no one excluded*. The Spirit's manifestation is given to *every believer* and is for every believer's profit. Thus, spiritual gifts benefit the entire Church and give believers some kind of supernatural advantage.

Another important word in this verse is "received." It is a form of the Greek word *lambano*, which is used more than 250 times in the New Testament, and it means *to receive into one's possession* or *to take into one's own control and ownership*. It carries the idea of *taking hold of something*, *grasping onto something*, or *embracing something so tightly that it becomes your very own*. This tells us that God — the Giver of spiritual gifts — wants each of us to *have* and *function* in His gifts, but in order to do so, we have to reach out and grab hold of the gift and begin to operate in it.

Scripture says we are to flow in the gifts, "...as good stewards of the manifold grace of God." The word "manifold" carries the idea of being *multi-faceted* — like the many facets of a diamond. When you put a diamond in the light, it begins to refract many beautiful colors as the light hits it from different angles. In the same way, the gifts of the Holy Spirit are many and manifest in many different ways. God doesn't want you to be like everyone else. He simply wants you to discover *your* gifts and begin to shine with the brilliance of His grace. And this is done from start to finish by *faith*.

QUESTION 2: Rick, have you ever seen anything supernatural, such as seeing into the spirit realm, seeing angels, or having a vision from God?

"Yes, I have. Many years ago, long before it happened, God gave me a vision that we were living and ministering in Russia. From that vision, I knew in my heart God was calling us to Russia to do the very things we are doing right now. I have also had an angel appear and speak to me about my ministry and what our family would be doing as a part of the end-time harvest. Now, I don't have visions and see angels every day or every week, but I have experienced these types of spiritual manifestations at pivotal moments in my life.

"The fact is, all of us should expect to see and experience things in the supernatural. We are living in the last of the last days, and the Bible says that God is going to manifest Himself powerfully during this time. Acts 2:17 says, 'And it shall come to pass in the last days, saith God, I will pour out of my Spirit upon all flesh: and your sons and your daughters shall prophesy, and your young men shall see visions, and your old men shall dream dreams.' So dreams and visions from God should be expected.

"Now, we need to know how to judge what we see and hear to determine whether it is from the Lord or from some other source — like the enemy or our own flesh. Sometimes we can have such strong emotional feelings in our soul about something that we mistake it for God's voice. So we really need to learn how to discern what we're hearing, which is why I wrote a book called *Testing the Supernatural: How To Biblically Test Dreams, Visions, Revelations, and Spiritual Manifestations*. It's a small but very helpful book that I highly recommend."

QUESTION 3: Can people really be translated in the spirit from one place to another?

It appears that more and more people these days are talking about being translated from one place to another. Can that happen? Yes, it can. The Bible gives us an example of this type of supernatural manifestation in the account of Philip meeting with and ministering to the Ethiopian ruler.

After carefully explaining a passage from the book of Isaiah to the Ethiopian, the Bible says, "And he commanded the chariot to stand still: and they went down both into the water, both Philip and the eunuch; and he baptized him. And when they were come up out of the water, the Spirit of the Lord caught away Philip, that the eunuch saw him no more: and he went on his way rejoicing. But Philip was found at Azotus: and passing through he preached in all the cities, till he came to Caesarea" (Acts 8:38-40).

What's interesting is that the words "caught away" in verse 39 is the very same Greek word used to describe the rapture of the Church in First Thessalonians 4:17. Without question, what Philip experienced was a supernatural work of the Holy Spirit, and while being transported from one place to another can happen, we cannot make it happen ourselves of our own will.

A careful study of both the Old and New Testaments reveals that when anything supernatural of this nature took place, no one was trying to force their way into the spirit realm. They were just living their life, when suddenly God burst onto the scene and did something phenomenal that only He could do — and what He did was ultimately for His purposes, not for the direct benefit of the individual.

Another example of this would be when Peter went up on his housetop to pray. It was just about noon, and the Bible says, "And he became very hungry, and would have eaten: but while they made ready, he fell into a trance" (Acts 10:10). The words "fell into" are a translation of the Greek word *ginomai*, which describes *something totally unexpected — something surprising that takes you off guard*. Peter didn't know he was going to have a vision; he was just waiting for his lunch to be prepared. But before he knew it, he was taken into the realm of the spirit where God corrected his view of the Gentiles and opened his heart to share the Gospel with people like Cornelius and his family.

Again, that's the way supernatural experiences take place — *suddenly*, *unexpectedly*, and by the will of God, not man. Be careful of anyone who says things like, "We're going to pry our way out into the spirit realm," or "We're going to force a supernatural experience to take place." That does not agree with Scripture.

[For more on this topic, please check out Rick's book *Testing the Supernatural.*]

QUESTION 4: Today many people seem to be speaking of supernatural visits to Heaven. Some pastors say this is biblical, and others say it's *not* biblical. What is your viewpoint?

When we look at Scripture, there are at least two documented visits to Heaven, and one was experienced by the apostle Paul. To understand what took place, we need to first look at what happened to him when he was ministering in the city of Lystra.

The Bible says, "And there came thither certain Jews from Antioch and Iconium, who persuaded the people, and, having stoned Paul, drew him out of the city, supposing he had been dead. Howbeit, as the disciples stood round about him, he rose up, and came into the city: and the next day he departed with Barnabas to Derbe" (Acts 14:19,20).

From this passage — and the one in Second Corinthians we're going to look at next — we understand that Paul did die, but when the believers encircled him and prayed for him, the Holy Spirit raised him from the dead!

What happened to Paul when he died? He talks about his experience in **Second Corinthians 12:1,2**:

> **It is not expedient for me doubtless to glory. I will come to visions and revelations of the Lord. I knew a man in Christ above fourteen years ago, (whether in the body, I cannot tell; or whether out of the body, I cannot tell: God knoweth;) such a one caught up to the third heaven.**

In these verses, Paul is modestly talking about himself and what he experienced. Apparently, there were other people boasting to the Corinthian believers about their supernatural encounters. Paul was not trying to impress the Corinthians or boast like the others; he was simply letting them know that he too had had a genuine, supernatural experience. Specifically, he said he was taken to the third heaven. He went on to say:

> **And I knew such a man, (whether in the body, or out of the body, I cannot tell: God knoweth;) How that he was caught up into paradise, and heard unspeakable words, which it is not lawful for a man to utter.**
>
> **— 2 Corinthians 12:3,4**

Here, for a second time, Paul said he was caught up into Heaven (paradise), and while he was there, he heard mind-blowing revelations. But he was not given permission to speak about or elaborate on what he heard.

The apostle John was also caught up into Heaven and was given the Revelation of Jesus Christ, which we have come to know as the book of Revelation. So being caught up into Heaven is biblical and it can certainly happen. You may have heard of someone today who has said they have experienced a trip to Heaven, and they very well may have done so. Nevertheless, in such matters we would be wise to be cautious of anyone who says they're going to Heaven every day or every week. There is no biblical example confirming supernatural experiences like these happen with such frequency.

[For more on this topic, please check out Rick's book *Testing the Supernatural*.]

QUESTION 5: Are there evil spirits over regions and cities? What authority do we have to pull them down and to do warfare against them?

Just as there is a visible world around us, there is also an invisible realm of the spirit. And in that unseen realm, there are God's angelic forces of good and Satan's forces of evil. In Ephesians 6:12, Paul tells us, "For we wrestle not against flesh and blood, but against principalities, against powers, against the rulers of the darkness of this world, against spiritual wickedness in high places." The description Paul gives us in this verse seems to reveal that at some point the Lord allowed him to see into the spirit realm to see how Satan's army is structured.

'Principalities' Are the Highest-Ranking Demons

The first category of underworld forces Paul names is "principalities." In Greek, this is the word *archas*, which was used symbolically to denote *ancient times, the very beginning*, or *the origin*. It was also used to depict *individuals who hold the highest and loftiest position of rank and authority*. It is the word for *princes* or *principalities*.

By using the word *archas* — translated here as "principalities" — Paul is telling us that at the very top of Satan's domain, there is a group of ruling demon spirits that are like *princes* or *principalities*, and they've held their chief positions of power since ancient times.

'Powers' Are Just Under Principalities

The second category of demonic forces we see is "powers." This is a translation of the Greek word *exousia*, which describes *delegated authority* or *influence*. This word denotes *one who has received delegated power* and is often translated *authorities*. Furthermore, the word *exousia* could also depict *those who wielded authority entrusted to them by their superiors*. These evil spiritual forces have received a license — or authority — to carry out all manner of evil and wickedness. They're like roaming spirits about the earth doing whatever they want to do.

'The Rulers of the Darkness of This World'

The next group of enemies from hell that we come up against is described as "the rulers of the darkness of this world." This phrase is a translation of the Greek word *kosmokrateros*, which is a compound of the words *kosmos* and *kratos*. The word *kosmos* denotes something *ordered* and *arranged*, and the word *kratos* describes *raw power*. When these words are compounded to form *kosmokrateros*, it describes *evil powers that have been organized and arranged against us*.

What's interesting is that this is the very word for *military training camps where young men were assembled, trained, and turned into a mighty army*. The new recruits were taught discipline and order, and all that manpower was converted into an organized, disciplined army. Thus, the word *kosmokrator* — translated here as "the rulers of the darkness of this world" — describes raw power that has been harnessed and developed into *a highly trained and aggressive force*.

The apostle Paul uses this word to tell us how serious the devil is about victimizing the human race. He takes demon spirits, which are like raw evil power, and trains them into organized forces. For example, there are demonic "rulers" that are exclusively trained to inflict cancer, induce addictions, and produce perversity. Once their training is complete, Satan sends them forth against us to steal, kill, and destroy anything and everything they can.

'Spiritual Wickedness in High Places'

Paul rounds out his list of evil spirits, describing a fourth level of demons he calls "spiritual wickedness in high places." The word "wickedness" is a translation of the Greek word *poneria*, which describes *destruction, disaster, harm, or danger*. It depicts something *malicious or malignant; foul, vile, hostile*, and *vicious*. "Wickedness" is not only that which is dangerous to the physical body but also that which is dangerous to the spirit or mind. This word *poneria* was also used to depict *animals that are savage, wild, vicious, and dangerous*.

Paul tells us these spirits of wickedness have been dispatched into "high places," which in Greek refers to *the lower region of the air*. Thus, these demons haven't been sent to Mars, Venus, or outer space. They're trafficking in our atmosphere, attempting to gain access and control of our lives.

God has given us powerful weapons to stand against and defeat all these demonic foes, and they're called the armor of God (*see* Ephesians 6:14-18). With these weapons — and the name of Jesus and His blood — we can take authority over the enemy and enforce the victory Christ died to give us.

[For more on this topic, please check out Rick's book *Dressed To Kill.*]

QUESTION 6: How can I detect a demon in someone I love and cast it out of him or her?

We need to understand that there's a difference between being demon *possessed* and being *demonized*. A person that is possessed would be someone who is totally under the control of Satan. They no longer have a will of their own, nor can they make their own choices. Although this level of demonic activity is certainly possible, it is not common.

When demonic activity is talked about in the gospels, it describes demonization. For instance, when the Bible says that Jesus healed many who were "possessed with devils," it uses the Greek word *daimonidzomai*, which describes *those that were demonized* or *those under the influence of a demon or group of demons.* Rather than total possession, this is extreme oppression by evil forces. Like Jesus, we can learn to recognize and cast out these foul spirits using the authority of His mighty Name.

[For more on this topic, please check out Rick's five-part series *What the New Testament Tells Us About Demons.*]

STUDY QUESTIONS

Study to shew thyself approved unto God, a workman that needeth not to be ashamed, rightly dividing the word of truth.
— 2 Timothy 2:15

1. After reading through all these supernatural-related questions and answers, which one made the greatest impression on you? Why was it so captivating?

2. The Bible teaches us that there are *fruits* of the Spirit and *gifts* of the Spirit. Take a moment to look up these passages and identify these supernatural manifestations that are for every believer.
   - **The Fruit of the Holy Spirit** – Galatians 5:22,23
   - **The Gifts of the Holy Spirit** – 1 Corinthians 12:4-11

According to Ephesians 6:14-18, what are the seven powerful weapons in the armor of God? What other mighty weapons has God given you to stand against and defeat the enemy? (*See* Revelation 12:11; Hebrews 9:14; Philippians 2:9-11; and John 14:13,14.)

PRACTICAL APPLICATION

> But be ye doers of the word, and not hearers only,
> deceiving your own selves.
> —James 1:22

1. Have you ever personally observed something supernatural? Has God ever enabled you to see into the spirit realm, see angels, or given you a vision of any kind? If so, share your experience.

2. Do you know of anyone who claims to have been translated in the spirit from one place to another? How does their experience support the biblical examples of Philip, Peter, and John? Does their experience ultimately fulfill *God's* purposes or serve to benefit the individual?

3. What has God called *you* to do? Do you know? How has He gifted you to represent Him and help others connect with Jesus? If you know your calling, how are you actively doing your part?

4. If you don't know what God has called you to do, take time now to pray and ask Him to reveal to you His purpose for your life.

LESSON 4

TOPIC

Questions About Prayer

SCRIPTURES

1. **Hebrews 6:12** — That ye be not slothful, but followers of them who through faith and patience inherit the promises.

2. **Hebrews 10:36** — For ye have need of patience, that, after ye have done the will of God, ye might receive the promise.

3. **Ephesians 6:18** — Praying always with all prayer and supplication in the Spirit, and watching thereunto with all perseverance and supplication for all saints.

4. **Daniel 10:12-14** — Then said he unto me, Fear not, Daniel: for from the first day that thou didst set thine heart to understand, and to chasten thyself before thy God, thy words were heard, and I am come for thy words. But the prince of the kingdom of Persia withstood me one and twenty days: but, lo, Michael, one of the chief princes, came to help me; and I remained there with the kings of Persia. Now I am come to make thee understand....

5. **Daniel 10:20,21** — Then said he, Knowest thou wherefore I come unto thee? and now will I return to fight with the prince of Persia: and when I am gone forth, lo, the prince of Grecia shall come. But I will shew thee that which is noted in the scripture of truth: and there is none that holdeth with me in these things, but Michael your prince.

6. **Ephesians 6:12** — For we wrestle not against flesh and blood, but against principalities, against powers, against the rulers of the darkness of this world, against spiritual wickedness in high places.

7. **1 Thessalonians 5:17** — Pray without ceasing.

8. **Galatians 6:7** — Be not deceived; God is not mocked: for whatsoever a man soweth, that shall he also reap.

GREEK WORDS

There are no Greek words included in this lesson.

SYNOPSIS

Prayer is not a duty — it is a *privilege*. It's an open-ended invitation to talk and commune with God, the Creator of Heaven and Earth, about absolutely anything that is on your mind. Just as a typical toolbox has many different tools to be used for all kinds of jobs, God has provided us with a spiritual toolbox that is equipped with several different types of prayer that are each designed for a specific purpose. Learning to use the right prayer at the right time — and how to "pray without ceasing" — are very important to having an effective prayer life.

The emphasis of this lesson:

Have you ever wondered why some prayers take longer to answer than others? Or how demonic forces can affect your prayers? Or what it actually looks like to "pray without ceasing"? Rick answers these questions

and also explains the blessings that are released when you take your eyes off yourself and use your efforts to be a blessing to others.

QUESTION 1: Why do some prayers take so long to be answered?

To answer this question, let's look once more at what the Bible says in Hebrews 6:12: "That ye be not slothful, but followers of them who through faith and patience inherit the promises." In this passage we see that it takes both *faith* and *patience* to inherit the promises of God. Faith is the initiator and is always acting and moving forward. And as we saw earlier, the word "faith" in Greek is masculine, and the word "patience" is feminine. Just as it takes a man and a woman to come together to produce a child, *it takes faith and patience to come together to give birth to the promises of God.*

Normally, when we believe for something and pray for it, we want it immediately. However, we're usually not ready to receive what we're asking for. Consider this example: If a woman became pregnant in one moment and then gave birth to her baby five minutes later, how do you think she would handle it? Can you imagine the super-accelerated experience of her body's chemistry changing and enlarging to accommodate the full development of a baby in minutes? How difficult might that be mentally, emotionally, and physically?

The time needed from conception to delivery is actually a *gift* to the expecting mother. She's pregnant, but she's not yet ready to receive her baby. In the same way, God often allows for a waiting period between our asking for something and then receiving it. He gives this time to prepare us on all levels for what He has prepared for us. The moment we release our faith, things are engaged and the answer is on the way. But *patience* is required to help us — and sometimes other key people — to be prepared.

Hebrews 10:36 says, "For ye have need of patience, that, after ye have done the will of God, ye might receive the promise." The word "patience" here is the Greek word *hupomone*, which is a compound of the words *hupo* and *meno*. The word *hupo* means *under*, as *to be under something*. The word *meno* means *to stay* or *to abide*. Therefore, this word "patience" is a picture of one who has resolved, "I'm not moving. I'm not budging. I'm not flinching. I don't care how heavy this load I'm under becomes; this is my spot, and I'm not surrendering or yielding it to anyone. This territory, this principal, this promise belongs to me, and I refuse to move."

What happens when you decide to become immovable like this? The devil is the one that moves. The fact is, he'll push you around as long as you let him. But the moment you stand still and resist him steadfastly in the faith, he starts retreating.

That's what the word "patience" means — *to remain in one's spot; to keep a position*; or *to resolve to maintain territory that has been gained.* It has been translated as *staying power* or *hang-in-there power.* It is *the attitude that holds out, holds on, outlasts, perseveres, and hangs in there, never giving up, refusing to surrender to obstacles, and turning down every opportunity to quit.* Essentially, "patience" (*hupomone*) is the Greek word for *endurance.* It is staying in a position of faith.

Keep in mind that there are different kinds of prayer. Paul confirms this in Ephesians 6:18, saying, "Praying always with all prayer and supplication in the Spirit...." The words "with all prayer" is a translation of the Greek phrase *dia pases proseuches,* and it literally means *with all kinds of prayer.* Just as Roman soldiers had many different types of lances they used in battle, Paul tells us that God has made many kinds of prayer available to us for different moments in our fight of faith.

The New Testament talks about seven different kinds of prayer, including the *prayer of consecration*, the *prayer of petition*, and the *prayer of authority*, which some people call the *prayer of faith.* Then there is the *prayer of thanksgiving*, the *prayer of agreement*, the *prayer of supplication*, and the *prayer of intercession.* Each form of prayer is very important and serves a different purpose from all of the others.

Again, think about a tool box. It has different tools for different tasks. If you try using a screwdriver to do the job of a hammer, it's not going to work. You need the right tool for the right task. In the same way, if you're praying the wrong kind of prayer for what you're facing, you might not get the results you need. You have to use the right prayer for the right situation.

With whatever prayer you use, it will always require patience. Again, Hebrews 10:36 says, "For ye have need of patience, that, after ye have done the will of God, ye might receive the promise." Make no mistake: part of God's "will" for you is to develop "patience" (*hupomone*) to stay in your place of faith so that you might receive His promises. Again, the word "receive" here is the Greek word *komidzo*, which means *to receive what is due or what one has coming to him.*

So if it seems like it's taking a long time to see God's promise fulfilled, don't be discouraged. Stay in faith. Payday is coming. If you'll keep believing and planting into patience, you'll see the promises of God become a reality in your life.

[For more on this topic, please check out Rick's five-part series *Different Kinds of Prayer.*]

QUESTION 2: Why did an angel in the book of Daniel fight with the prince of Persia for 21 days before that angel finally appeared to Daniel?

The account in the book of Daniel regarding an angel fighting with the prince of Persia is a perfect example of the spiritual warfare we sometimes experience in prayer. As chapter 10 opens, Daniel is in mourning and has been fasting for three weeks. Then suddenly, an angel appears to him and begins to speak to him saying, "…Fear not, Daniel: for from the first day that thou didst set thine heart to understand, and to chasten thyself before thy God, thy words were heard, and I am come for thy words" (Daniel 10:12).

Isn't that interesting? The moment Daniel began to pray, an angel of God was dispatched in answer to his prayers. But something happened that hindered God's answer from getting through to Daniel. The angel told him, "But the prince of the kingdom of Persia withstood me one and twenty days: but, lo, Michael, one of the chief princes, came to help me; and I remained there with the kings of Persia. Now I am come to make thee understand…" (Daniel 10:13,14).

What was keeping the answer to Daniel's prayer from getting to him? A *principality* ruling over the kingdom of Persia was blocking it from reaching him. The angel went on to tell Daniel, "…Knowest thou wherefore I come unto thee? and now will I return to fight with the prince of Persia: and when I am gone forth, lo, the prince of Grecia [Greece] shall come. But I will shew thee that which is noted in the scripture of truth: and there is none that holdeth with me in these things, but Michael your prince" (Daniel 10:20,21).

We Are in a Spiritual Battle

These passages in Daniel unquestionably confirm the nature of the fight we're in. As we saw in Lesson 3, the Bible says, "For we wrestle not against flesh and blood, but against principalities, against powers, against the rulers of the darkness of this world, against spiritual wickedness in high places" (Ephesians 6:12).

The word "principalities" is the Greek word *archas*, which is where we get the word *archbishop*. This word was used to denote *ancient times, the very beginning*, or *the origin*. In this case, it indicates *fallen angels and evil powers that have held the highest and loftiest position of rank and authority since the very beginning of time*. The *archas* — translated here as "principalities" — are at the very top of Satan's domain, and they're to be dealt with by God's angelic forces.

Our focus in spiritual warfare is primarily "...against spiritual wickedness in high places" (Ephesians 6:12). In Greek, the term "high places" refers to *the air below the mountain tops*. God's angels deal with everything *above* the mountain tops, and we deal with what is below the mountain tops, which is the atmosphere where we live and breathe. That's where demons have been dispatched and where they fight fiercely, attempting to gain access and control of our lives.

Thank God we have been given the blood of Jesus, the Name of Jesus, the Word of God, and the gifts of the Holy Spirit to deal with and defeat the enemy. Indeed, "...The weapons of our warfare are not carnal but mighty in God for pulling down strongholds" (2 Corinthians 10:4 *NKJV*).

[For more on this topic, please check out Rick's book *Dressed To Kill*.]

QUESTION 3: In your teaching "7 Things to Do Every Day to Stay Spiritually Strong," you talk about developing a life of daily prayer. Can you please give an example of what this looks like and how to get started?

In First Thessalonians 5:17, we are instructed to "Pray without ceasing." In the original Greek, this means to *pray without a pause, pray without intermission*, or *pray without a break*. Basically, "pray without ceasing" means that prayer literally becomes a *lifestyle*.

Rick shared this insightful snapshot from his daily life as an example:

"When I get up every morning, I begin to pray before I ever lift my head off the pillow. Why? Because we're told in Psalm 5:3, 'My voice shalt thou hear in the morning, O Lord; in the morning will I direct my prayer unto thee, and will look up.' Before my feet hit the floor, I begin going through a mental list of people, and I pray for them. These include my family, all of our partners, and all of our viewers.

"After I get out of bed and put on my robe, I walk into the kitchen and I turn on the coffee maker. I then do my morning push-ups, get my cup of coffee, and make my way into the room where I read my Bible and pray. As I'm opening my Bible, I say, 'Holy Spirit, please show me wondrous things out of Your Word today.' That's a prayer right out of Psalm 119:18, which says, 'Open thou mine eyes, that I may behold wondrous things out of thy law.'

"I then read and pray simultaneously — going from reading to praying and praying to reading. I encourage you to do that as well. After I read a verse, I'll say, 'Holy Spirit, help me understand that verse better.' And He does!

"Friend, prayer is not a ritual. It is an ongoing, unbroken conversation that flows from our heart. What's interesting is that among the people of God in Israel, they believed every gesture was a prayer. That's why even today when you go to the Wailing Wall in Jerusalem, when the Jews pray, they're moving their entire bodies as they speak to God. In their minds, that's what it means to worship God with all their mind, their soul, and their body.

"Personally, I believe every tear we cry and every movement we make is a prayer. Prayer is everything you *are*, and it's everything you *do*. I believe that's what the apostle Paul means when he said, 'Pray without ceasing' (1 Thessalonians 5:17). Simply make a decision to develop a mindset that you're going to live in a state of prayer, and ask the Holy Spirit for the grace to do it. *You can do all things through Christ who strengthens you* (*see* Philippians 4:13)."

[For more on this topic, please check out Rick's five-part series *Seven Things To Do Every Day To Stay Spiritually Strong*.]

QUESTION 4: Do you think the modern-day Church, or at least in Western culture, is hyper-focused on what God can do for us? For example, are we too focused on success, prosperity, and answered prayer and not focused enough on what we can do for God or His Kingdom?

Generally speaking, most of the Church in the Western culture does tend to be very self-focused and self-absorbed. This is actually more a result of the age in which we're living rather than the Church itself. The Bible tells us that one of the primary signs of the last of the last days — the days in which we are now living — is that "...men shall be lovers of their own selves..." (2 Timothy 3:2).

If all we do is sit around and think about ourselves, our world becomes pretty small. But when we begin to focus our mind on what we can do for others and how we can give to help someone else hear the gospel and see the Kingdom of God advance, suddenly our life begins to rapidly enlarge. The more you reach beyond yourself and your world, the bigger and more fulfilling life becomes.

If you think about it, everything ties to the principal of *sowing and reaping.* If you go through life day in and day out with a mindset of, "I want to reap, I want to reap, I want to reap," eventually you're going to stop reaping altogether. In order to reap — and keep on reaping — you have to become a *planter.* In other words, you *live to give* rather than live to get.

If you want love, then begin to *give love.* If you want attention, then begin to *give attention.* If you want time, begin to *give time.* If you want mercy and forgiveness, then begin to give *mercy* and *forgiveness.* Everything in life is like a seed that we sow, and the ground we sow into is other people's lives. What you do for others and for the Lord is what's going to be done for you.

God's Word is clear: "God will never be mocked! For what you plant [sow] will always be the very thing you harvest. The harvest you reap reveals the seed that you planted" (Galatians 6:7,8 *TPT*). In the original Greek text, the verb tense here could literally be translated, "Whatever you sow and sow and sow and sow, that is what you will reap and reap and reap and reap." If you will develop a life of sowing, you will also develop a life of reaping.

Are we still "word of faith people"? Yes. We believe in receiving everything that God has promised us in His Word, but we also need to think about how we can be a blessing to others. On a regular basis, we should pray, *Lord, please help me get my mind off of myself and onto You and others. Help me see who needs love. Show me how and where I can sow my time, talent, attention, and money. In Jesus' name. Amen.*

[For more on this topic, please check out Rick's book *A Life Ablaze.*]

STUDY QUESTIONS

Study to shew thyself approved unto God, a workman that needeth not to be ashamed, rightly dividing the word of truth.
— 2 Timothy 2:15

1. After reading through these questions on prayer, what stood out and challenged you most?

2. When it comes to the hierarchy of Satan's evil forces, who are the *highest* ranking demons? Who are the *lowest* ranking spirits? Which ones are we assigned to deal with, and who has been designated to fight the other evil forces?

3. The New Testament talks about seven different kinds of prayer: the *prayer of consecration*, the *prayer of petition*, the *prayer of thanksgiving*, the *prayer of agreement*, the *prayer of supplication*, the *prayer of intercession*, and the *prayer of authority*, which some people call the *prayer of faith*. Which of these forms of prayer are you familiar with and can describe? Which one (or ones) have you used most?

4. In your own words, describe what it means to *pray without ceasing*? How does the example of prayer from Rick's life help you understand this principle and better assimilate it into your own life?

PRACTICAL APPLICATION

But be ye doers of the word, and not hearers only, deceiving your own selves.
— James 1:22

Regrettably, most of the Church in the Western culture tends to be very self-focused and self-absorbed, and as a result, the lives of many believers have become quite small and unfulfilling. How about you? Where do you rank when it comes to reaching out and meeting the needs of others? Get quiet before the Lord and ask Him to help you honestly answer these self-evaluating questions:

- *What kinds of things fill my thoughts, prayers, and conversations? Am I focused on me, or God and others?*

- *When I look at my calendar, where am I spending the bulk of my time? On me, or God and others?*

- *When I look at my bank statement or checkbook, where am I spending my money? On me, or on God and others?*

- *How often do I think about helping someone else? When was the last time I actually did something for someone else?*

Based on your answers above, what can you do to begin *living to give* instead of living to get? Pray and ask the Holy Spirit to enlarge your world and "…Be mindful to be a blessing, especially to those of the household of faith [those who belong to God's family with you, the believers]" (Galatians 6:10 *AMPC*).

LESSON 5

TOPIC

Random Questions

SCRIPTURES

1. **Mark 9:48** — Where their worm dieth not, and the fire is not quenched. [*Hell is a place where the worm never dies, and the fire is never quenched.*]

2. **Luke 16:25** — But Abraham said, Son, remember that thou in thy lifetime receivedst thy good things, and likewise Lazarus evil things: but now he is comforted, and thou are tormented. [*Hell is a place of regretful memories.*]

3. **Luke 16:26** — And beside all this, between us and you there is a great gulf fixed: so that they which would pass from hence to you cannot; neither they pass to us, that would come from thence. [*Hell is a place*

from which those who die in sin can never depart once they have gone there.]

4. **Revelation 9:2** — And he opened the bottomless pit; and there arose a smoke out of the pit, as the smoke of a great furnace; and the sun and the air were darkened by reason of the smoke of the pit. [*Hell is a great furnace.*]

5. **Revelation 14:11** — And the smoke of their torment ascendeth up for ever and ever: and they have no rest day nor night, who worship the beast and his image, and whosoever receiveth the mark of his name. [*Hell is a place where its inhabitants can never find rest.*]

6. **Psalm 116:3** — The sorrows of death compassed me, and the pains of hell gat hold upon me: I found trouble and sorrow. [*Hell is a place full of eternal pain and destruction.*]

7. **Proverbs 27:20** — Hell and destruction are never full; so the eyes of man are never satisfied. [*Hell consumes lost souls like a beast whose hunger is never satisfied.*]

8. **Mark 5:8-13** — For he said unto him, Come out of the man, thou unclean spirit. And he asked him, What is thy name? And he answered, saying, My name is Legion: for we are many. And he besought him much that he would not send them away out of the country. Now there was there nigh unto the mountains a great herd of swine feeding. And all the devils besought him, saying, Send us into the swine, that we may enter into them. And forthwith Jesus gave them leave. And the unclean spirits went out, and entered into the swine: and the herd ran violently down a steep place into the sea, (they were about two thousand;) and were choked in the sea.

9. **2 Timothy 3:1, 3** — This know also, that in the last days perilous times shall come… [People will be] without natural affection, trucebreakers, false accusers…

10. **1 Corinthians 10:14** — Wherefore, my dearly beloved, flee from idolatry.

11. **1 Corinthians 10:32,33** — Give none offense, neither to the Jews, nor to the Gentiles, nor to the church of God: Even as I please all men in all things, not seeking mine own profit, but the profit of many, that they may be saved.

GREEK WORDS

There are no Greek words included in this lesson.

SYNOPSIS

There is a broken piece of granite that can be found on the Renner Studio TV set, and it is significant because it was once a part of the foundation of the massive statue of communist-leader Felix Dzerzhinsky — a statue that is no longer standing. Dzerzhinsky was the KGB leader during the days of Stalin, a time when persecution in the Soviet Union was fierce. But this tyrannical monster that terrorized all of Russia is no longer in power. This fragment of granite is a tangible reminder of the fulfillment of Scripture that says *God is in control*!

The Bible says, "But God in heaven merely laughs! He is amused by all their [the nations'] puny plans. And then in fierce fury he rebukes them and fills them with fear" (Psalm 2:4,5 *TLB*). Friend, regardless of what rulers say or do, God is still in charge! The fact is, "There is no [human] wisdom or understanding or counsel [that can prevail] against the Lord" (Proverbs 21:30 *AMPC*).

The emphasis of this lesson:

In this lesson, Rick explains why Jesus talked so much about Hell and why we hear so little about it today, and why He gave the demons that were controlling the demoniac permission to enter the pigs. You'll also learn the right way of changing church membership, what God thinks about divorce, and whether it is right or wrong for a believer to drink alcohol.

QUESTION 1: I've heard that Jesus spoke frequently about hell and warned people about it. *Did* Jesus actually speak a lot about hell — and, if so, why do we hear so little about it today?

Jesus *did* speak about hell frequently. In fact, hell was the number one subject He talked about. He was fully aware of hell's existence, and He wanted everyone to know it was a real place so they would choose not to go there. The gospels are full of statements Jesus made regarding hell and what it is like.

Jesus said hell is a place...

- *Like a great furnace* (Revelation 9:2).

- *Where those who die in sin go and can never depart once they've gone there* (Luke 16:26).

- *Where the worm never dies, and the fire is never quenched* (Mark 9:48).

- *Where regretful memories are always in the minds of its residents; they remember everything they did and every opportunity they had to repent and receive Christ but rejected it* (Luke 16:25).

- *Where its inhabitants are tormented day and night and can never find rest* (Revelation 14:11; 20:10).

- *Full of eternal pain and destruction* (Psalm 116:3).

- *That consumes lost souls like a beast whose hunger is never satisfied* (Proverbs 27:20).

It should also be noted that hell was never intended to be inhabited by people. Jesus said it is a place of "...everlasting fire, prepared for the devil and his angels" (Matthew 25:41). As a matter of fact, the Lord prompted the prophet Ezekiel to write, "'...As I live,' says the Lord God, 'I have no pleasure in the death of the wicked, but that the wicked turn from his way and live...'" (Ezekiel 33:11 *NKJV*). Clearly, it is God's greatest desire for "...all men to be saved and to come to the knowledge of the truth" (1 Timothy 2:4 *NKJV*).

Why do we hear so little about hell in the Church today?

Probably the biggest reason hell is not talked about is because many people don't believe it exists. Pew Research Center conducted a study in 2014 and found that while 72 percent of all adults in the U.S. believe there is a heaven, only 58 percent believe there is a hell. What's also surprising is that only 70 percent of Christians believe in hell. That means 30 percent — nearly one-third of those who call themselves believers — don't believe there is a literal hell.

Many pastors avoid the subject because they don't want to make people feel uncomfortable. Likewise, many people really seem to struggle to believe that a loving God would create such a horrible place and allow people to go there. This is why many times when a sinner dies, people are very reluctant and uncomfortable to talk about the possibility that their friend or loved one didn't make it into Heaven. They hope with everything inside of them that somehow that person's good works outweighed their bad behavior and that they were right with God when they died.

Nevertheless, if we believe the Bible, than we know that *unless* a person confesses with his mouth that Jesus is Lord and believes in his heart that God raised Him from the dead, he is not saved (*see* Romans10:9,10). Presently, it is estimated that nearly 150,000 people die every day worldwide. That means every second, about two people slip into eternity, and according to Jesus, many of them are heading for hell. In Matthew 7:13 and 14, He said, "…Wide is the gate, and broad is the way, that leadeth to destruction, and many there be which go in thereat: because strait is the gate, and narrow is the way, which leadeth unto life, and few there be that find it."

The fact that Jesus said hell is a real place and many people are headed there should jolt us into thinking more about eternity. The people we see at the grocery store, at the mall, and in restaurants are all eternal beings that are going to spend eternity somewhere. May the Holy Spirit help us to be mindful of others and ready to share the Truth with those around us who are looking for hope.

[For more on this topic, please check out Rick's book *A Life Ablaze*.]

QUESTION 2: Why did Jesus give the demons in the demoniac leave to enter the swine in Mark 5?

Immediately after crossing the Sea of Galilee, Jesus and His disciples got out of their boat and were met by a man with an unclean spirit (*see* Mark 5:1,2). The Greek actually says that this man was *in the grip of an unclean spirit* or *in the control of an unclean spirit.* Therefore, this man didn't have an unclean spirit; *the unclean spirit had him.* He was literally in the grip and control of an unclean spirit.

The word "unclean" in Mark 5:2 is the Greek word *akathartos*, and it means *unclean, impure, filthy, lewd, or foul.* Unclean spirits are so filthy and impure that they will live anywhere — even among the death and decay of a graveyard. Somehow, someway, this demon gained entrance into this man and created an infestation of uncleanness inside him.

The Bible says Jesus confronted this demon directly and said, "…Come out of the man, thou unclean spirit" (Mark 5:8). What's interesting is that the Greek tense in this verse actually indicates that Jesus *kept saying over and over and over,* "Come out of him, come out of him, come out of him."

Apparently, the demon was initially resistant to surrender and obey Jesus' command.

Normally, when the Lord cast demons out of someone, He did it with a single command. Just one word from the lips of the Master, and the demons vacated. But when we come to this account in Mark 5 (also recorded in Matthew 8:28-34 and Luke 8:26-39), we see that the demon wouldn't budge. Instead of giving up and walking away, Jesus stayed and grew more determined to see this man freed. He kept *saying* and kept *saying* and kept *saying*, "Come out of the man."

The demon's resistance led Jesus to ask, "…What is thy name? And he answered, saying, My name is Legion: for we are many" (Mark 5:9). Jesus wanted to know why the unclean spirit wouldn't budge, so He asked its name. "Legion," the demon snarled back, "for we are many." The word "legion" is the Greek word *Legion*, which is *a military term that denoted at least 6,000 Roman soldiers*. By using the word "legion," the unclean spirit was saying, "You're talking to me, but there are 6,000 of us inside this man." This brings us to the phrase "we are many," which in Greek is *polloi semen*, and it means *we are many in number, we are a multitude, we are a vast number*.

After the demon gave its name and revealed how many other evil spirits were with him, the Bible says, "And he [the demon] besought him [Jesus] much that he would not send them away out of the country" (Mark 5:10). The word "besought" here in Greek means *to beg, request, beseech, or pray*. Basically, the unclean spirit in this man began praying and begging Jesus not to send them out of the region.

Scripture goes on to say, "Now there was there nigh unto the mountains a great herd of swine feeding. And all the devils besought him, saying, Send us into the swine, that we may enter into them" (Mark 5:11,12). Where did the demons ask to go? Into a herd of "swine," which *in this verse is the plural form for a pig or hog*. Swine were considered to be *the lowest, basest, and most unclean of animals*. According to the Law, Jews were not to have anything to do with pigs — they shouldn't have even been in the area.

Notice that it says "all the devils besought" Jesus. Up until that moment, one demon had been speaking to Jesus as the spokesman. But suddenly the situation shifted from one demon doing the talking in verse 10 to *all the demons* pleading with Jesus in verse 12. Imagine the sound of 6,000 devils all speaking simultaneously, begging to be sent into a herd of pigs.

Demons desire to live in something, and if they can't inhabit a person, they will live in an animal, such as a dog or a pig. "And forthwith Jesus gave them leave. And the unclean spirits went out, and entered into the swine: and the herd ran violently down a steep place into the sea, (they were about two thousand;) and were choked in the sea" (Mark 5:13).

The Greek actually says "they were choking as they went into the sea." In other words, the demons were strangling the pigs as they drove them into the water. The reason this is important is because when these 6,000 demons were living in *one man*, the man was still alive. Even though they had tried multiple times to get him to take his life, they were unsuccessful. In fact, when the man saw Jesus get out of the boat, he was able to exercise his will and run to Jesus for deliverance.

Animals, such as the herd of 2,000 swine, don't have a will. Therefore, the moment the demons went into the pigs, they went crazy and were immediately driven to destruction. That is the purpose and mode of operation for evil spirits — they seek to steal, kill, and destroy whatever they can. Jesus sent the 6,000 demons into the herd of pigs to teach us what the devil will do if he is allowed to have his way.

[For more on this topic, please check out Rick's five-part series *What the New Testament Tells Us About Demons.*]

QUESTION 3: How should I change church membership?

There is a right way and a wrong way to change your church membership. The *wrong* way would be to just up and leave the church you've been attending without giving any notice to anyone. Imagine if you were the pastor and someone you had been pouring into and watching over for weeks, months, or years just suddenly disappeared, and then you heard not long afterward that they were attending another church. How would that make you feel?

The Bible says that pastors have the responsibility to watch over your soul and will actually give an account to God for what they do (*see* Hebrews 13:17). If you feel that you are to go to another church, at least have the courtesy and respect to tell your pastor. This is the *right* way to change your membership, and it will keep your pastor from wondering where you are or what has happened to you. A good pastor will want to know where the "sheep" that are under his care are and how healthy they are spiritually.

And by all means, if there's something wrong in the church that he needs to know about, you owe it to him and the rest of the church to respectfully and lovingly share your concerns. A good pastor will want to listen and hear what you have to say, and if you still want to leave, he should not try to stop you.

QUESTION 4: Does God always hate divorce?

In Second Timothy 3:1, the apostle Paul wrote, "This know also, that in the last days perilous times shall come…." Then in verse 3 he told us that people will be "…without natural affection, trucebreakers, false accusers…." The phrase "without natural affection" is from the Greek word *storgos*, which describes *a devotion and commitment to one's family*. In this case, however, an "a" has been added to the front of the word, forming the new word *astorgos*. This depicts *a lack of devotion or an absence of commitment to one's family*; it is *the deterioration of family relationships* or *the loss of family affection*. By using this word, the Holy Spirit was prophesying through Paul that at the very end of the age, there will be a breakdown and deterioration of the traditional family and the home. This is exactly what we're seeing take place all around us in epic proportions.

There was a time during Jesus' ministry that the Pharisees tested Him on the subject of divorce, asking Him if it was lawful for a man to divorce his wife for just *any* reason. "And He answered and said unto them, 'Have you not read that He who made them at the beginning "made them male and female," and said, "For this reason a man shall leave his father and mother and be joined to his wife, and the two shall become one flesh?" So then, they are no longer two but one flesh. Therefore what God has joined together, let not man separate'" (Matthew 19:4-6 *NKJV*).

Indeed, it is God's desire that husbands and wives stay together for life, because divorce always has tragic consequences for the couple as well as the children. If it is possible, it is in everyone's best interest to seek good, godly counsel and work together to reconcile the marriage. It is true that in some situations, divorce is unavoidable. If that is the case, follow God's instructions through Paul in Romans 12:18 (*AMPC*): "If possible, as far as it depends on you, live at peace with everyone."

[For more on this topic, please check out Rick's 15-part series and his book *Last-Days Survival Guide*.]

QUESTION 5: Is it right or wrong for a believer to drink alcoholic beverages? Some seem to believe it's okay as long as you don't get drunk, and others believe it is a sin. Can you answer this please?

Statistics show that addictions in the world today are off the charts. The Bible strongly urges us to flee the temptations that come our way. In this day and age, all kinds of temptations seem to abound at every turn — especially addictive temptations such as alcohol.

Writing to the believers at Corinth, the apostle Paul said, "Wherefore, my dearly beloved, flee from idolatry" (1 Corinthians 10:14). At the time Paul wrote this, idolatry was inseparably linked with fornication and drunkenness. When pagans came into pagan temples to seek relief from the pain and pressures of life, it was customary for the priests to mix hallucinogenic drugs together with alcohol and give it to the pagan worshipers. The priests would then send the worshipers home, ensuring them that everything would be alright. But after the temporary relief from the drugs wore off, the pagan worshipers were no better off, and in some cases they were worse. The only thing that they knew to do to get relief was to return to the pagan temple for more alcohol and drugs. Hence, a cycle of dependency or addiction was born.

There is much stress and many pressures in the world today, and people often turn to alcohol to numb the pain. Likewise, medications, drugs, sex, and even excessive eating have all become things people reach for to cope with life. The bottom line is, we need to be very careful not to become dependent on anything but God. That is what Paul meant when he wrote, "All things are lawful unto me, but all things are not expedient [appropriate]: all things are lawful for me, but I will not be brought under the power of any" (1Corinthians 6:12).

Now look at this same verse in *The Message*. It says, "Just because something is technically legal doesn't mean that it's spiritually appropriate. If I went around doing whatever I thought I could get away with, I'd be a slave to my whims." This brings us to another very important point regarding drinking alcohol. You may feel like you have the liberty to take a social drink every now and then, and it has never been a problem for you. But what is it doing to the people around you who are watching your life? How is it affecting them?

Think About the Spiritual Health and Wellbeing of Others

Interestingly, just a few verses after Paul tells us to "flee from idolatry" and to "not be brought under the power of anything," he said, "Give none offense, neither to the Jews, nor to the Gentiles, nor to the church of God: Even as I please all men in all things, not seeking mine own profit, but the profit of many, that they may be saved" (1 Corinthians 10:32,33). Essentially, Paul is saying, "You need to be thinking about the spiritual health and wellbeing of others. Don't cause someone else to stumble and fall into sin by your example."

Friend, if you're living your life only focused on yourself and your rights, something is not right. However, if you live your life with sincere concern for others, answers to questions like "Do I drink, or do I not drink?" will become clear to you.

[For more on this topic, please check out Rick's five-part series *How To Successfully Divert and Overcome Temptation*.]

We pray this series of questions and answers has been helpful for you and strengthened your relationship with the Lord. He loves you more than words can say and has promised to be with you always. May you experience a fresh revelation of His indescribable love for you as you continue to abide in Him!

STUDY QUESTIONS

Study to shew thyself approved unto God, a workman that needeth not to be ashamed, rightly dividing the word of truth.
— 2 Timothy 2:15

1. When was the last time you heard a message on the subject of hell? Why do you think it is crucial for all believers to have a fresh revelation of this place of eternal torment — especially in these last days?

2. What new eye-opening facts did you learn from the story of Jesus and the demoniac? What does the fact that a legion — 6,000 demons — were living inside one man say to you about a person's spiritual capacity?

3. Carefully read the full conversation between Jesus and the Pharisees concerning divorce in Matthew 19:1-9 (also in Mark 10:1-12). For what reason did Jesus say divorce was permitted? What was the Pharisees' real problem that Jesus exposed?

4. When the pressure is on and life is overwhelming, what do you reach for to cope with life? We need to be very careful not to become dependent on anything but God, which is one reason He prompted Paul to write the same instructions *twice* in his letter to the believers at Corinth. Pause a few moments to reflect on First Corinthians 6:12 and 10:23 and write what the Holy Spirit speaks to you in these verses.

PRACTICAL APPLICATION

> But be ye doers of the word, and not hearers only,
> deceiving your own selves.
> — James 1:22

1. It's estimated that every second, nearly two people slip into eternity, and according to Jesus, many of them are heading to hell. It's no wonder the Holy Spirit urges us to "...Be ready at all times to answer anyone who asks you to explain the hope you have in you" (1 Peter 3:15 *GNT*). Are you ready to respectfully share with others the reason you've made Jesus your Lord and Savior? If you had 60 seconds to tell someone that you knew was dying about Jesus, what would you say? Pray and ask God to give you a brief testimony you can readily share with others.

2. You may feel like you have the liberty to take a social drink every now and then because it's never been a problem for you. But what's it doing to the people around you who are watching your life? How's it affecting them? Consider carefully what God is saying in these verses:

    He who heeds instruction and correction is [not only himself] in the way of life [but also] is a way of life for others. And he who neglects or refuses reproof [not only himself] goes astray [but also] causes to err and is a path toward ruin for others (Proverbs 10:17 *AMPC*).

    Now we who are strong ought to bear the weaknesses of those without strength, and not just please ourselves. Each of us is to please his neighbor for his good, to his edification. For even Christ did not please Himself... (Romans 15:1-3 *NASB*).

Let no one then seek his own good and advantage and profit, but [rather] each one of the other [let him seek the welfare of his neighbor] (1 Corinthians 10:24 *AMPC*).

What is the Holy Spirit showing you about your *personal responsibility* to others in these passages? (Also consider Paul's words in Romans 14:13-21 and Philippians 2:1-4.)

Notes

Notes